Modern Artists   Masson

Harry N. Abrams, Inc., Publishers, New York

Otto Hahn

Masson

4

No World Is Complete is the title of a painting by André Masson—it is also his aesthetic, his way of looking at the world, his ethics. Each of Masson's works is in this way a question and the sketch of an answer—What is life? What are joy, happiness, abundance?— Each is a question that opens perspectives, that closes them. Each of Masson's paintings traces out the movement of a thought, all of his paintings challenge each other back and forth in a Hegelian progression. Every step calls into being the step after, for there is no place to take refuge, every pause signifies death. Masson must therefore burrow into his private labyrinth at the risk of losing his way, and this is why Ariadne's thread plays such a role in his work; Ariadne's thread which becomes a tangled skein, a cord like a length of bowel whose course reveals the labyrinthine circuit of the organic world. (The labyrinth from which he strives to extricate himself is, perhaps, nothing more than that which traps every man.) Masson's work is therefore convoluted, overlapping itself layer upon layer, and any explanation of it is often no more than another enigma. To understand Masson one must trace the road he has taken through the years. But most of all we must know what truth he seeks, and discover what words like life, joy, ecstasy, and movement mean to him. We must ferret out what concrete experience hides behind those mere words.

But this is not easy, for Masson never speaks of his beginnings. His childhood seems simply not to exist for him—as is true, in general, of all men who live in what they aspire to become rather than in what they once were. It may be that he passed through his childhood entirely divorced from himself, in the transparent contemplation of what surrounded him. Then, as with most contemplatives, the desire to dissolve, to become one with the universe, was little by little, toward the years of adolescence, transmuted into a feeling of frustration. Incapable of possessing the world, he felt himself cheated by it.

The fact that Masson has rubbed out his childhood is in itself important: he has no desire to bring to light the emotions of his first years, he feels no nostalgia for a past which might enshrine the ultimate image of happiness. And for this reason he has no place where he can luxuriate, hide himself, or rest.

When he does dwell on his life, he never goes back beyond that contemplative adolescent possessed by an exaltation and a dionysiac intoxication at the spectacle of nature. At sixteen, he borrowed his vocabulary and the shape of his dreams from Nietzsche. At nineteen, his bottled-up energy clamored for an outlet. The war had just broken out. He had no hatred of the enemy, no holy mission to reconquer either Alsace or Lorraine. Patriotism meant nothing to him, and yet he returned from a settled life in Switzerland so as not to miss an adventure great enough to satisfy his appetite for danger and for the dizzy heights of living.

From a life lived only in dreams and books he found himself suddenly thrown into the front lines, into a world of excrement and torn bodies, plunged into the obscenity of men deprived of women who exorcise their fear and hopeless lust by burying love under loathsome words. He lived, belly on the ground, in the no man's land of assault troups, huddled in shell holes or behind corpses. It was there he discovered that two thousand years of civilization have taught us nothing, that barbarism still exists in man; humanity is therefore never really achieved, and one must never put his trust in human nature. This is the despair that haunts Masson's work.

But beyond this lesson, meditation in the midst of filth and rot brought to him an even more horrifying revelation: neither reason nor morality can prevent man from finding in the contact with death a grandeur, an intoxication to satisfy his most delirious dreams. Man is irresistibly fascinated by blood, by filth, by murder. Power-drunk, thirsty for the sublime, ecstatic in his delusions of grandeur, man loves destruction and fear, desires his own death and the death of others. This has nothing to do with his intelligence or morality; even common sense is no help. The irrational erupts into life and turns topsy-turvy all the good notions.

This then was the terrifying discovery Masson made and which sapped forever all of his confidence in human reason. From then on he was to refuse all systematic thinking, any political pigeonhole, for he realized that sadism and barbarity can at any time govern man's behavior: the blood baths of antiquity are echoed by medieval cruelties, reborn in the monstrous acts of Nazism, and continue in the horrors of colonialism. It is no accident of the human condition that there are torturers, criminals, hangmen. The forces of irrationality lie everywhere, waiting. Even when they are backed up by some political system, it is at mankind that they point the accusing finger.

André Masson, like Antonin Artaud, has accepted the burden of declaring aloud that man is a sadist. The sadistic side of man must be faced squarely, for he is prone to forget it, and when he does collective assassinations are the result. And after each flood of hatred, we absolve human nature and put the blame on the system; the notion of mankind regains its lost purity without our ever having to admit that, whatever the system, uncontrollable forces always threaten to burst forth anew.

Masson experienced this irrationality the day a bullet ripped into his chest. He remained on his feet, standing still, unconscious of pain. The world around him became something wondrous and he experienced his first complete physical release, while in the sky there appeared before him a torso of light. Joy in the challenge drove out fear, and there remained in him only an irrational desire to come closer to the light-drenched torso of death. "I fear nothing any more," he said to himself, "I am dead; the greatest of human adventures has happened to me. . . ."

Frozen where he was, still on his feet, he had to be flattened on the ground by a fellow soldier. During the wait for the stretcher-bearers, who did not venture near the front line until nightfall, he lay cramped in a shell hole alongside the mummified cadaver of a German. (Later, Masson always referred to it as "Rameses II.")

Then began the long succession of hospitals, fits of rage, revolts, refusals to accept treatment, and finally the psychiatric hospital where he was confined. Through this, he dreamed of fleeing Europe, of taking refuge in the Indies, where life moved at a different pace.

The war scarred him deeply and was apparently responsible for his fundamental experience: it grafted disorder onto the desire for total possession and the feeling of frustration which had lingered on from his contemplative childhood. The art of Masson was to be a meditation on this disorder. What is life? How can one take possession of the world in a joyous exaltation? How does one live to the fullest? These are the questions he seeks to answer through painting, for with him the problems life poses and those set by creation are inseparable. Sartre has summed up this unity very well: "For Masson, the will to paint is not distinct from the will to be a man." Thus, even before his meeting with the Surrealists, who turned this notion into a dogma, Masson conceived of painting as a *way of knowing*.

Emerging from the war shattered and incoherent, subject to sudden fits of rage, he should, by all rights, have turned out painting which mirrored his inner disorder. To expect this is to forget that through painting Masson has always sought a way, a style of living—building a man and devising art constitute a single process for him. Terrorized by chaos, he sought a remedy for it. On the verge of madness he looked to reason. Because life unfolds itself in anarchy, there must be a hierarchy of values, space itself must be put into order. Thus, he chose Derain as his first teacher. He set out on a series of *Forest* pictures—majestic trunks soar high (*Trees*, page 30), images of serene grandeur, of equilibrium, in pale colors with delicate nuances.

7   From these first paintings, Masson's method was to be that of a dialogue. His fundamental experience having been of disorder, he

sought to overcome it, to go beyond it, unlike a main current of modern painting which seeks its solutions in a return to childhood. Klee, Chagall, and Miró confine the world in a bubble of dreams floated up from the depths of their childhoods. They have domesticated their world; it becomes a thing of charm, clownlike, a child's toy. This current seeks the truth by giving emphasis to emotions captured at the very moment of their birth, and can be considered a kind of expressionism.

The artistic second current, that of the Impressionists and Cubists, looks for its truth in the total possession of the world and in the dialogue between emotion and reality. "How can you get a table onto a canvas?" the Cubists ask themselves. With Picasso, Braque, and Matisse there is no deliberate slipping back to childhood. They seize the world with an adult's eagerness and simply take for granted their childhoods' contributions to present experiences. This is the line to which Masson adheres: he wishes to grasp life with a grown man's desires. Rather than looking to childhood for consolation, he seeks to dominate. For Masson, in that first period of his painting, an ideal existence would be like a forest astir with presences, peopled by immense human creatures, entirely developed and fully visible, reaching toward heaven. Calm, majesty, and order are the virtues Masson extolled then.

But when disorder had been overcome, frustration reappeared, for equilibrium always ends in repetition and immobility. As a reaction, Masson strove to seize the world, to penetrate into the cyclone's eye. His trees begin to take on life, to bend before the storm (*Storm*, page 31). Branches break and fall. Far off the sea booms; in the foreground a grave opens.

The *Card Players* (page 32), painted around this same time, reveals the same feeling. The perspective adopted by the painter dominates the table; on it are jumbled hands and cards over which heads lean. The viewer's gaze plunges down on them and is projected toward the four corners of the canvas. The scene is taken in as a whole, a dynamic totality supported by a circular movement.

Thus began Masson's evolution as a painter, an evolution sparked off by frustration and disorder and transformed into a restless quest perpetually challenging what has gone before. He seeks an architecture, an order; then, once found, he resents as a constraint the armature intended to support the expression and promptly casts it off, plunging into a new exploration destined to end in the same finding and rejecting.

Here then is his pattern: he seeks some certitude, he finds it and establishes it, but then it casts a shadow—suggests a counter-proposition—and the idea splinters and becomes confused, leaving the painter once again face to face with his own disorder. Later

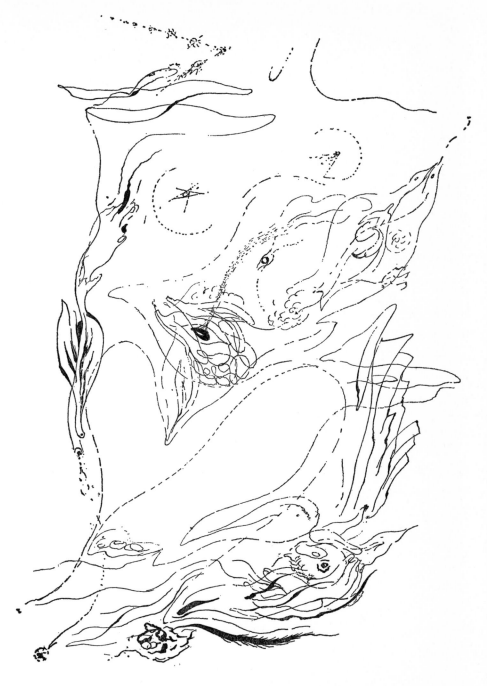

la naissance des oiseaux.

he was to title one of his works *The Demon of Indecision*—two similar profiles facing in opposite directions. This twofold split takes on many forms. In a whole series of pictures there appear together a preconceived plan and an automatic drawing whose cohabitation reveals a double desire—to surrender to the wave of existence, to tame the whirlwind. In order to go beyond this opposition, Masson has been impelled to bring about those moments in which the personality recovers its unity: moments of joy, love, ecstasy, intoxication, and even of that terror in which the body, invaded by fear, grapples with emergencies unaided by the brain.

In 1924, at the same time he sought a release for his vital energy, he called reality itself into question. His still-life paintings (*Italian Postcard*, page 33), hitherto quite orderly, became complicated through an effort to integrate several planes of reality: an antique statue is introduced into the composition, then a postcard, and that same postcard is reflected in a glass, thereby lending a new ambiguity to the real. Where is the truth of it? In art, as represented by the statue? In the photograph? In the reflection of that photograph? Or in the totality of these various elements? This heaping of image upon image is in the tradition of Raymond Roussel,* whom Michel Leiris brought one day to Masson's studio to buy a painting in which there was precisely this, a single image worked out on several planes of reality.

By these means Masson sought mental depth while remaining on the surface of the canvas. About the same time, at Plestin-les-Grèves, he painted an "interior" in which a half-open door opens onto a vestibule from which one glimpses other half-open doors. This kind of exploration of space proved unfruitful, and Masson decided to destroy the painting.

The concept of space toward which he was moving was not based on depth but on the kind of movement exploited in the *Card Players* and on the windstorms that sweep the *Forest* series. He searched for that space which separates the photograph from its reflection, which links art to reality. He ransacked his personal world of images, and one day the torso of light revealed to him at the moment he was wounded found its way onto a canvas (*Armor*, page 34).

Rational order capsized and the ordered structure with which he so often begins his paintings cracked apart. In 1924 he painted a man clambering out of a crumbling structure. The work was purchased by Antonin Artaud, who was beset by the same problems as

---

* French writer and poet (1877–1933). An eccentric and mysterious character much admired by Marcel Duchamp, the Surrealists, and, lately, by the partisans of the New Novel. His unusual work is a labyrinth of images containing all the formal possibilities of an unrestrained imagination.

Masson. Both felt themselves crushed by civilization, and both looked to irrational forces to liberate man from the iron yoke which weighs him down, imprisons him.

Thus, after his initial rejection of the irrational element, Masson surrendered himself to it. The dizzy heights of delirium, titanic intoxication, the rage to destroy, to slash to shreds, to seize, to swallow up—all these are found also in love, in the contemplation of a landscape, in every act of life.

For Masson Surrealism represented the leap into the irrational. When he came into contact with the group led by André Breton, Masson brought to it a furious unleashing of unconscious forces. His first Surrealist works gave free rein to his imagination, and his paintings were transformed into dream cloths floating in space above solid constructions (*Dead Man*, page 35). Objects are often indicated by only a few lines, by a stroke of the hand which sets them in flight. Soon even this pretext is dropped and the hand is set free, guided only by the need to express an inner tension. These are the first automatic drawings, of which Masson was to do some two hundred, almost all of them abstract. The constraints of representation sloughed off; they are no more than moving lines tracing a labyrinthine circuit. Then hands and breasts are introduced haphazardly, and the only importance of such details is in what they imply; they can be positioned anywhere because they are carried on a whirlwind's swirls (Automatic drawings: *Birth of the Birds*, page 9; *Lovers*, page 11).

Masson is revealed in the uncontrolled steeplechase of his automatic drawing. His "inner rhythm" asserts itself: it is his willful surrender to the whirlwind, a whirlwind that becomes a labyrinth which closes down and sucks in, provoking the desire to wrench oneself free, to liberate oneself. This is the origin of the theme of flight, of the wing. From whatever angle Masson approaches his subjects, he always ends up with the notions expressed in his automatic drawings: delirious germinations complicated to the point of becoming nothing more than labyrinthine tangles of vegetable, organic, or mental circuits. When later he had recourse to graphic signs, they, too, proliferated to become whirlwinds snatching bodies into their eddies, and these eddies in turn gave rise to an undertow of mysterious forces out of which mutations arose.

The technique of automatic drawing lures time into a trap. An Impressionist painting is tied precisely to the position of the sun (in Monet's landscapes one can tell the hour of day). With Masson, time proliferates, dissolves; it is simultaneously a momentary vision and a slow unfolding, a transformation, both "before" and "after" caught together: a hand appears in one place and pops up elsewhere. Using this automatic technique, Masson was the first to give a form to that space conceived in the mind where time decomposes, multiplies, becomes entangled, where right and left are confused, where up and down are one and the same, where the center ceases to exist (*Pursuit*, page 36; *The Great Fish Battle*, page 37).

Masson's sand paintings are the translation into pictorial terms of the spontaneity of his automatic drawings. *Death's Head* (page 39) and *Figure* (page 41), painted in this manner, preserve the linear technique of the drawings: glue is squeezed from the tube to make lines and tracks directly on the canvas. Instinctively Masson found it best to lay the canvas flat on the floor, as many abstract painters were to do later. This Action Painting technique, in which the entire body is involved in the art work, is an ideal medium for Masson, who neither aspires to lock up the world in a precious coffer labeled Art nor desires to set anyone at ease by his work. Since nothing in the painting ever existed before, everything must be conquered for the first time. Eager to possess the world, Masson is obliged to embrace the entire universe. It is in this will to seize it all, to extend himself, that the unity of the multiple facets of his art must be sought. It is an art that begins with trials and blind groping and ends in discovery, and then suddenly, just when the style has been fully realized, he smashes it all, recoils, and launches again on the quest for a new form.

In the process of perfecting a style, his way of laying hold of reality, Masson may think that in such and such a way he can succeed in catching the world in the trap of painting. But once the style has been perfected, the very perfection of the tool reveals that this is not the means that will permit him to grasp the world and the truth.

Masson is not searching for a style, a pictorial procedure. As soon as he recognizes that from a perfect style he gets only a perfect painting but not life itself, he discards that style and looks for another. In this he is an orthodox Surrealist: art is a way of knowing and not the fabrication of a dream world. However, it was precisely because of the split induced by this thirst for lyric possession that Masson came into open conflict with André Breton. Breton, confident of his superiority, held aloof from the world and was prone to withdraw into himself disdainfully. He could not therefore understand Masson's attitude, any more than that of Artaud, since both men had need of the world to realize themselves, to project themselves into it. Both Masson and Artaud desired to take hold of the world for purposes of conquest, to rip from it that vital force so reluctant to yield itself. This caused the schism between Breton and them.

13   Masson's first post-Surrealist works mark a new beginning. The compositions are more static, and it is color—which appears for the

first time—that is called on to breathe lyricism into the work and to express tension. The gestures of the personages become blurred and play the same role as the whirlwind in the automatic drawings.

From 1930 to 1936 Masson tackled a great variety of themes: young girls wringing the necks of chickens and plucking them, sleepers, slaughterhouses, massacres, bullfights, landscapes, and insects. In these works—all of them like explorations—the same concerns turn up over and over again: the clash between man and animal, the clash between feminine sweetness and the sadism of domestic activities. Only the man asleep (*Sleeper*, page 42) knows peace; he is suspended in floating sheets of color.

The *Massacres*, which for many years were Masson's principal theme, have no moral lesson to preach. No more than there is any center in Masson's conception of space is there any moral aim in his pictures. The *Massacres* series is related to the brewing ferment of the automatic drawings, to the colored exhalations of the *Emblematic Landscapes* (*Ibdes de Aragon*, page 43), to the atmosphere in which the *Sleepers* dissolve. The people of the *Massacres* are plunged into a milieu (the formal and moral concerns of Masson come together in the notion of "milieu"), into a bath of violence, an atmosphere at the same time horrible and sublime—struggle for existence or cycle of nature (*Massacre*, page 15; *Massacre*, page 45). There are neither good nor evil men, only men who tear each other apart, who smash and destroy. An equivocal lyricism sweeps through them, as it does through the pictures of the insect world, hatching mad tangles out of which sprout sadistic mutations: claws transmute themselves into tongs, mandibles into scythes, into knife blades, chitinous dry bodies shrivel into skeletons, into armor. And along with them, rocks are metamorphosed into men, stones into heads, and in the *Bullfights* series the bull becomes woman crushed by man, or man who receives the *estocada* from death itself.

In the satirical drawings of the Spanish Civil War, Masson found a means of returning to his aggressive lyricism—priests transformed into crowned asses, soldiers with bulls' muzzles, landscapes littered with cadavers which pullulate like stones (*Not Enough Earth*, page 17).

In 1937 Masson returned to France. A period of synthesis began in his work, in which he went back over everything he had acquired in the preceding years. He started with a few paintings that pin down the environment, take possession of the premises, so to speak. Then he threw himself into a re-exploration of his themes and styles of the past fifteen years—the forests of his first works, sand paintings, Spanish landscapes, combatants, pursuits. He went through all his work and picked up the loose strands: 14

the rocks of Montserrat become men and women, the figure of a man strikes us suddenly as strange, like one of the warriors of 1927; a woman changes into an egg, the egg becomes a shellfish, while the warrior is reduced to a skeleton and then into a phantasmagoric donkey. It was at this point that the labyrinth made its entry into Masson's universe, along with its cortege of myths and symbols. A drawing of the period shows a Minotaur in a labyrinth; Ariadne's thread twists and tangles like a long loop of bowel that will end by strangling us all.

This was Masson's second Surrealist period, for the war in Spain had reconciled him with Breton. Although it began as a re-capitulation, this period slowly condensed everything that had preceded it. What previously had developed from one picture to another now little by little was compressed into a single work, at first as mere juxtaposition (as in *Ophelia* of 1937) and then as an internal metamorphosis within the work itself.

His brush followed his thought in revealing hidden meanings, but as fast as the knots were untied, the unraveled thread twisted again into an inextricable skein. The *Anthropomorphic Furniture* series (*Pygmalion*, page 46; *The Louis XVI Armchair*, page 47) is one of the high points in Masson's production. Here he rebuilds on a mental plane the labyrinth of the automatic drawings, the fortress-labyrinths which close in on and suffocate the Minotaur (*Labyrinth*, page 49): the chair becomes a praying mantis, the mantis is metamorphosed into a trap, the trap into a woman, the woman into a shellfish, until at last the chair is trap, shellfish, woman, and insect. Such chains of analogies weaving infinite nets are the essence of the thought process through which we comprehend a woman's flesh as the petal of a rose, a rose as a dewdrop, a dewdrop as spring itself. This is a new form of the theme of the pursuit, which dates back to the painter's initial confusion, for if the world is caught in a net, the net closes on anyone who pursues appearances, since there can no more be an end to the striving after total possession than there can be to thinking itself.

After the fine series of *Anthropomorphic Furniture*, Masson applied the same mental process to a cycle of imaginary portraits of Kleist, Heraclitus, and Goethe (*Portrait of Goethe*, page 50). Then he went to Martinique, where the style of the satirical drawings of Spain reappeared, developing the same device of image within image, this time in the form of delirious voluptuous vegetation: a tree becomes a hand, a hill a thigh, and so on.

What is Masson trying to convey by this proliferation of ambiguous meanings? Is it the visual expression of anxiety, of a poetic vital force? All of this, certainly, but above all it is *comprehension*, which for Masson is indistinguishable from the lyrical intoxication

« Les yeux de terre ! »
André Masson
1936

17

of supreme domination and which, in his development, subsumes all previous themes—pursuit, the thread of Ariadne, architecture at the same time necessary and fatal, tangled skeins punctuated by magnificent blossomings, labyrinths, floods of violence, knowledge drowning in its own profusion (*In the Tower of Sleep*, page 52).

Much has been said (and by Masson most of all) of germination and metamorphosis. Such terms apply only too well to Masson's work, but often they block any deeper inquiry. It is not transformation in itself which interests the painter, but the power—at once perilous and poetic—which sweeps through the elements of his painting and drives them where it will, for that power does not manifest itself except at the price of a mutation soaked in sadism. To be swept along in such intoxication the body must first undergo a metaphysical change: it is through becoming wolflike that man acquires terrific force, and to uproot himself from earth he must open his arms like spreading wings. This is the energy and supreme drive that excite Masson's will to live to the fullest. Later he was to seek this dynamic expansion in the teeming bursts of symbols and the shattering of colored space inscribed by lines like whiplashes.

Energy and mutations are inseparable. In the *Furniture* series, the *Portraits*, the *Minotaur*, and the drawings done in Martinique these two elements are taken up again on varying planes—mineral, vegetable, organic (*Being and Nothingness*, page 19). But with the first pictures painted in America, the perspective changes. In order to control the lyric explosion, Masson draws closer to the source, seeking to pin it down at its origin as dynamism, as tensions clamoring to burst forth but still unripe. In *Spring*, *Egg*, and *Painter in Meditation* he sets up a blueprint for a world in formation. This culmination of the painter's process in virtual abstraction is inseparable from both the realism of the period of 1930–36, in which Masson's new vocabulary was compiled, as well as from the synthesis that began in 1936. In this American phase, all the elements of preceding periods reappear—the earth seen at very close quarters, landscapes built out of vapors, insects, blossomings.

Masson's progression is perfectly clear: the paths he took in 1934–35 in a series of paintings come together in the works of 1938. *The Painter and Time* (page 53) and *In the Tower of Sleep* (page 52) from that year are good examples of that evolution. Masson gathers together all of his past, compressing it each time into a single painting. From one compression to another he makes his way back to the source, until finally, in America, he arrives at that essential force bursting with myriad possibilities. These vegetable or organic proliferations having been fully condensed, there remains only a swirl of abstract forms, subterranean gestations on the

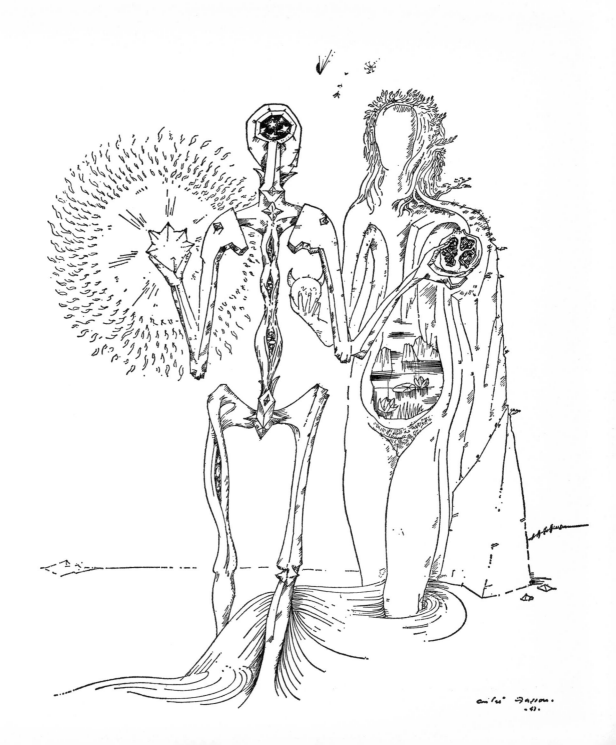

brink of eruption, as in *Pasiphaë* (page 55), in which all elements are reduced to essentials, so that the painting reminds one of a stained-glass window caked with mud through which only the most brilliant light can penetrate. Even this swirl is condensed, and by 1943 it is reduced to a dance of colored symbols filling the canvas. By 1944 nothing remains but lines of force (*Bison on the Brink of a Chasm*, page 21), infusing with rhythm a space in which colors explode (*The Sybil*, page 51).

These sheets of color in which symbols hover are the result of the earlier pieces of furniture being metamorphosed into plants whose color vibrations have now become pure colors, whereas the twisting of tropical lianas within their vegetal tangles have been refined to essential drawing.

The American period came to a head in this division between drawing and painting (*Elk Attacked by Dogs*, page 56).

Back in France, Masson for a while gave free rein to his basic drive. Well into 1946–47 there is still the obsession with earth, as in *The Burrow* (page 57), which exploits the subterranean glimmers of light of the *Germinations* series, but in a new context, in which the central concern is with atmosphere. This launched a new period, in which he makes use of space like a storm of color. Each time he settles in a new place, Masson needs to anchor his vision by concentrating on the new architectural element. Staking out his hold in this way, he takes his bearings almost as if by a topographical survey of the terrain, as in the *Forests* of 1922 and 1936, the emblematic Spanish landscapes, and the Martinique pictures. Upon his return to France, he painted first *La Sablonnière*, then *La Rochelle* in 1947. It was at that moment that he began to look toward Turner and the Impressionists; the symbolic lines and forms which lent rhythm and unity to his colors began to disappear, to be replaced by the vibration of the colors themselves. Landscapes became something like great heaving sighs traversed by colored puffs of air. Along with the drawn lines, the tragic element likewise dwindled away; life was no more than a serene dissolving, a fusion with the luminous atmosphere (*River in Autumn*, page 58). In 1949 he went so far as to speak of "Monet the Founding Father," thereby emphasizing the tradition he was returning to.

Now atmosphere pervaded the entire canvas; the horizon was pushed back, swallowing up landscapes and precipices. Color spread out like a liquid sheet, and water became a familiar theme—cascades, women bathing, rain. Onto Impressionism—one of whose sources was Japanese prints—Masson grafted a new Oriental element drawn from Zen philosophy: everything participates in movement, there is a continuity between the breast of the swimmer and the eddies of the wave.

From year to year the angle of Masson's vision widened, and the panorama tended to become a vast landscape swept by a sheet of

uniform color—rain falling on a mountain chain or inundating a valley (*Nocturnal Panorama*, page 59). This extension of the atmosphere led to the disappearance of forms, since distance effaced their contours, diluted their lines, drowned the color so that it inclined to uniformity. Because of this, Masson was led to take up again the graphic symbols abandoned five years earlier, symbols that served above all to people the monochromatic immensity of a swarm of trees, of a multitude of crests.

With color reduced little by little to mere tint, to a floating airy wash, its place was taken by these calligraphic signs, which increasingly came under Oriental influence. For more than a year Masson explored the possibilities of Oriental ideograms and their various combinations, culminating in the *Migrations* series (*Migration III*, page 61), in which the two aspects—vast space and graphic symbols—are brought together. In *The End of Summer*, *Animal Labyrinth*, and *Abyss* (page 60) the symbols devour the space entirely.

Up to the end of 1958 Masson pursued his conquest of new techniques, which return to and develop further the experiments of 1927. Little by little color returned to his painting. Thus, between 1946 and 1958 Masson went through a phase similar to that of 1930–36, concentrating on winning a new language and new territories. In 1959 he began a new period of synthesis, in which automatic drawing, Oriental calligraphy, color, space, and the notion of image within image are all taken up again and unified into a single expression, an expression of apparitions and of sudden upheaval. *Fertile Night* (page 63) and *Sorcerers* (page 66) are typical of this period. No attempt is made to organize the abstract whirlwind of cosmic forces. Instead, their rhythm is exploited and from it surge forth mythical figures. *Men and Chrysalids* (page 67)—the title itself evokes the idea of transformation—reveals the endeavor to inscribe a dynamic figure within a dynamic space. Unlike this period, the American phase was, as it were, under the sign of the chrysalid, of the cocoon, where all forces are interior, hidden. Toward 1960, after an interlude of disquieting impressionism and Oriental calligraphy, these forces burst forth again in a cosmic tornado that whirls up and sweeps along with it a universe of anthropomorphic symbols.

All his life Masson has striven to abolish the distance separating mental processes from art. His various techniques have all served the single purpose of minimizing the domination of the creator over his work. But in this endeavor to possess the world by means of art, intelligence is of no help. Knowledge never succeeds in completely exposing a subject, for it is always possible to take up again some detail in order to follow through its implications and refine its plastic quality.

Thus, the approach which stakes everything on *knowing* never ends up in anything. Cézanne had already faced up to the falsity of this pursuit: analysis splits reality into small parcels, atomizes it to the point of dispersion, in which stands unmasked the futility of all efforts to grasp reality. In this connection, Masson reports a conversation with the philosopher Heidegger, who confided to him: "Cézanne was no philosopher, but he understood everything about philosophy. He summed up in a few words everything I struggle to express. He said, 'Life is terrifying.' And that," Heidegger added, "is all that I have been saying for the past forty years."

In the work of Cézanne, Masson comprehends fully the consternation, the panic fear of a man who, after a hundred and fifty or two hundred sittings, still cannot finish a painting. If Masson is sensitive to this striving after an inaccessible reality, it is because he too experiences the same incapacity to complete a canvas in a normal state of mind: his lucidity pushes back all limits and drags him into a quest without end.

To tear himself free from this contemplation, he was led, even before his first Surrealist period, to seek some other means of contact—ecstasy or intoxication—which would lift him out of his fear and permit him to become one with his work in a kind of visionary rapture. But such a state, in which the mind works beyond thought, cannot be prolonged. It demands of the artist a frenetic speed. Automatism and rapidity become indispensable factors in this way of working.

An essential part of Masson's activity, automatism and speedy execution are typical not only of the series of automatic drawings but also of all his various phases from the early *Bucking Horses* to the sand paintings, from the *Massacres*, whose swift lines slash through space like lightning, to the drawings using ideograms, the calligraphic paintings, the *Migrations*, the *Women Multiplied* of 1957, and the *Magical Bodies* of 1961.

Rapid execution goes hand in hand at times with abundant production. Once, in a single day, Masson turned out twenty-two drawings on the theme of Desire (page 25) in order to exploit his inspiration to the fullest and to tear from it every possible meaning. In such feats Masson takes painting out of its formal limits to make it a vital force unleashed upon the world.

But speed in itself is not enough for him; the painter himself must enter into his picture, must fuse the painting and the act of painting. This is clearly indicated in the series *I Paint*, *The Painter and Time*, *I Draw Dante*, in which a hand pushes its way into the picture itself. But for such a projection to occur, the canvas must become a receptacle, a milieu into which both painter and viewer can plunge.

Masson was therefore led to transform the surface of a painting into a homogeneous environment in which one can soar, dissolve, float—an environment like water, like dreams, in which we levitate and loop the loop without ever falling, like the musical space in which the listener is bathed. The picture becomes a space to live in whose center is everywhere, in which right and left melt into each other, where high and low are one and the same.

This space-environment in which one can circumambulate in all directions is already fully present in *The Great Fish Battles*, in the automatic drawings, and in the *Massacres*, which are not descriptions of imaginary scenes but baths of violence in which gestures drift, spreading to the four corners of the canvas, as in the *Card Players*. Following these, the Spanish landscapes become effluvia, the American landscapes baths of earth, the atmospheric landscapes baths of luminous space, and today each painting reveals this same conception of space-environment, this same pulsation of ecstasy which strives to integrate the viewer into the lyric pool of the painted surface.

In this, Masson once again joins Antonin Artaud. Neither cares to address himself to lucid intelligence or to esthetic pleasure. Both wish to act through the body, by communicating a physical experience, by plunging the spectator into a paroxysm in which his body becomes perceptive entirely apart from his mind. It is the difference between an intelligent warning against some danger by merely describing it and the ear-piercing shriek of alarm which freezes us with fear. Explanations are directed to our reason, but the whole body understands the cry. It is this carnal contact with the cry that Masson seeks when he transforms the canvas into a space shot through with pulsations, into an environment which welcomes and sustains our delirium.

Even if conceived with no concern for any aesthetic, the work once finished becomes an aesthetic form subtended by formal structures. Because of this, the exponents of Action Painting were able to find in Masson's work the syntax of gestural painting, for which he had already laid down all the laws:

Lay the canvas flat on the floor.
Paint with movement of the whole body.
Seize your inspiration in that state of ecstasy and paroxysm in which mind and body coincide and regain their lost unity.
Let execution be a lightning-swift and automatic act.

Conceive space as a totality without center and without clues to orientation; then the canvas will become cosmic space, an expanding universe and—because there are no landmarks—a spatial trap.

Think of creation as a risk to be taken and of the picture as a commitment and an adventure.

This is Masson's immense contribution on the formal plane. It is a contribution inseparable from his personal human and psychological approach to life, inseparable from his own work taken as a whole.

The same preoccupations which gave rise to his automatic drawings crop up in every phase of his work, although Masson has always tried to work out each phase in a different way. Nevertheless, this diversity itself is consistent with Masson's logic. He was the first to visualize a work as the quest for a solution, as an adventure in which every step must be endured without ever stopping at or overdoing a style once it is achieved, but always pressing forward toward the solution. This insatiable desire to exhaust all technical possibilities is often held against Masson. And yet Masson has gone through fewer periods than Picasso, with whom he shares the idea that the painter's job is to embrace everything.

But whereas Picasso keeps a kind of daily diary of his emotions, ideas, and moods, Masson blazes landmarks along the trail of his thought. Herein resides their fundamental difference. For Picasso, painting is a quintessential means of seizing the world and dominating it; he belongs to a generation still confident of the power of art. Masson, however, is part of the generation which calls painting itself into question and which grants value to it only to the extent that it is linked to life and acts upon life. Masson knows that once the work is finished he remains behind, empty-handed. So once again he must join battle, once more throw himself into painting in the hope of plunging through to life. Nothing is more alien to Surrealism than the exploitation of a formula, of a manner. Masson has sought neither that paltry bunch of flowers called "personality" nor a self-limiting style. Because he aims at becoming one with the universe, his personality can only be the conquest of the whole. For this reason his work is not a "genre" of painting, but the trajectory of a spirit ceaselessly reaching outward.

In his lifelong forward march we can see that whatever technique Masson used, it was used only as a tool, and that at no point has he ever reneged. From the start there has been a perfectly logical and complete development:

1. From 1922 to 1929 first by means of a cerebral Cubism and then through Surrealism, Masson pushed experiments in drawing to the extreme point at which hands and feet could be positioned anywhere.

2. From 1930 to 1936 he concentrated on forcing colors to their highest intensity.

3. From 1936 to 1947 he achieved a synthesis between drawing and color.

In America, his drawing became form itself, and the colored forms absorbed all the colors, leaving only a black background. Drawing assimilated light and space ceased to exist. But the synthesis was doomed to destroy itself, having arrived at a contradiction. In order to liberate color, Masson concentrated the original black into drawn lines, which then became sign-drawings, since they took the place of forms. After this complete disintegration he began a new series of researches, during which drawing disappeared and was replaced by the pure luminosity of the background.

4. From 1947 to 1953 Masson further emphasized luminous space, until there was no longer even a hint of contrast. Finally, there remained only a monochrome wash, tinting the background.

5. From 1953 to 1958 Masson returned to his sign-drawings and wrung every possibility from them. These graphic symbols could take on any meaning—a marching column in the *Migrations* series, a dance gesture, human figures, vibrations. *Abyss* (page 60) is made up of a number of superimposed heads—or perhaps they are simply the motion of the sea, or maybe the bustling of a street.

6. Beginning in 1958, after having pushed his experiments with drawing and color as far as possible, Masson set out on a new period of synthesis.

What form will this new synthesis finally take? For the present we are still too close to it to make out a general line. Masson's most recent work—of August, 1964—seems to dip back into all the past cycles. At the same time static and dynamic, the picture first reveals an idol, then little by little new images emerge: a man and a woman who lift up an egg-shaped stone where a couple is fighting. Above, to the left, there is a "massacre." Image merges with image to create a subterranean germination like those of the American period, thereby bringing all of his past work up to date again.

It may be that Masson had to complete his entire trajectory before we could grasp the coherence of his course, before we could discover that the reeling vortex of his automatic drawings differs in no way from the atmospheric dissolution of 1947, that the "torso of light" of 1924 became the *Giants* of 1947 (page 25), that the *Massacres* of 1933 broke out again in the *Delirium—Lansquenet* of 1963 (page 69). Throughout his work the same themes crop up again and again: pursuit, combat, trap, labyrinth, explosion of architecture.

And always there is the double movement: domination of chaos, surrender to it. The precarious equilibrium never comes to rest. Even today, Masson envisages with the same anguish the further evolution of his art, as if something compels him with each new painting to throw a bridge across the void, to explore new solutions.

Marcel Duchamp said recently that modern painting had reduced art to a mere retinal emotion. "But there is more to art than that," he pointed out, "there are many other ways of conceiving creation." Completely in control of his painter's reflexes, André Masson has conceived his art as a means of knowing. Seen in this perspective, his work reveals its basic coherency and calls on us to follow the development of an art whose pace is set by the artist himself, a man who drives relentlessly ahead.

29

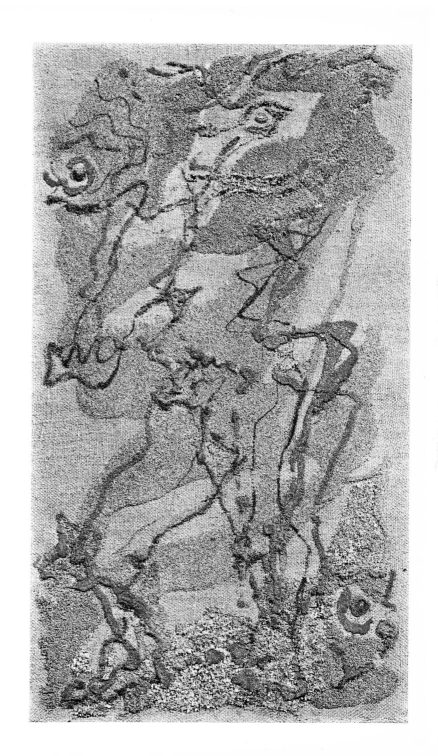

41

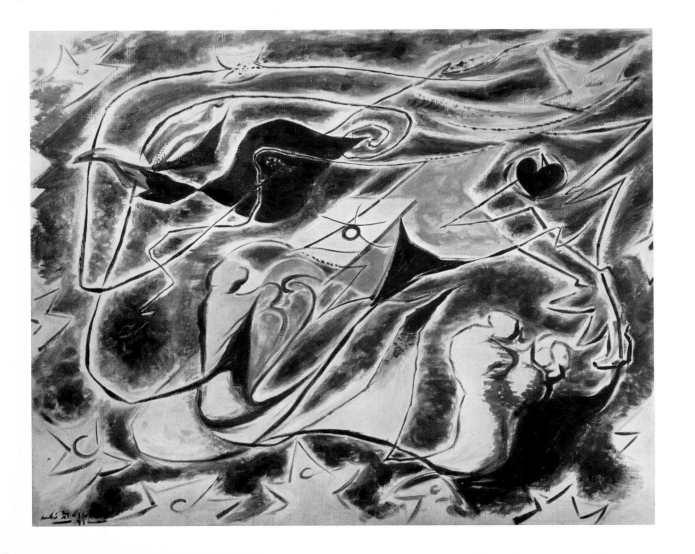

42

47

51

58

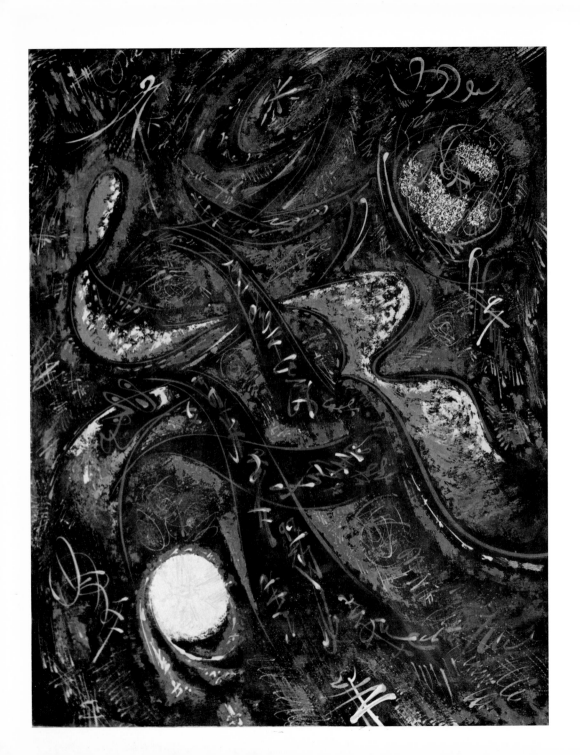

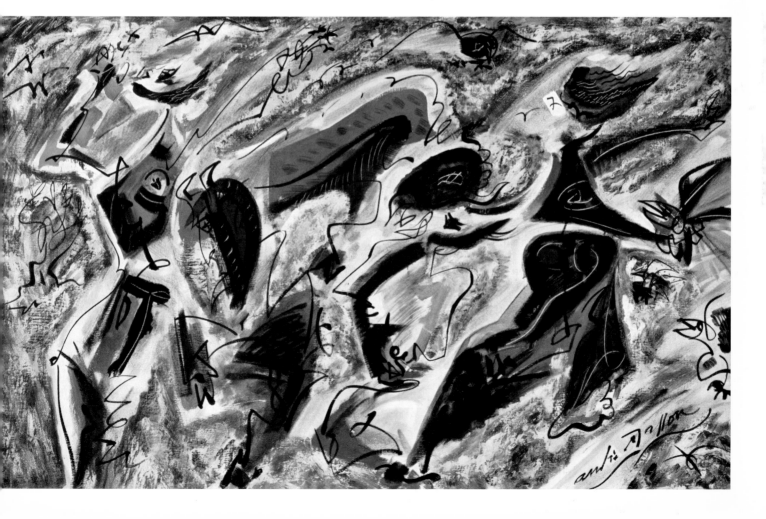

66

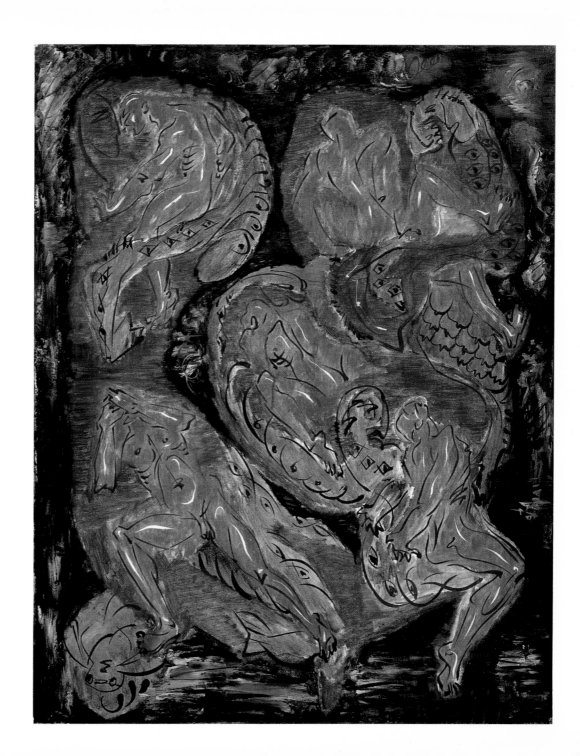

Biography

1896	January 4: born in Balagny (Oise), France
	Studies at the Académie Royale des Beaux-Arts in Brussels and the Ecole des Beaux-Arts in Paris. Studies fresco painting under Paul-Albert Baudouin
1914	Journeys to Italy and Switzerland. Military service; severely wounded
1919	With the sculptor Manolo in Céret (Pyrenees)
1922	Moves to Paris. Contract with Daniel-Henry Kahnweiler, Galerie Simon. Friendships with Joan Miró and the poets Armand Salacrou, Michel Leiris, and Georges Limbour
1924	February: first exhibition at the Galerie Simon, opened by Georges Limbour. Meets André Breton, Louis Aragon, and Paul Eluard. Joins the Surrealists and takes part in their exhibitions
1924–30	Lives in Nemours (Seine-et-Marne), Antibes (Alpes-Maritimes), and Sanary and Dattier (Var). Journeys to England, Holland, and Germany
1930	*Lovers* series. Paul Rosenberg buys pictures
1932–33	*Massacres* series
1933	Breaks definitively with the Surrealists. Stays at the Lac des Settons (Morvan). Scenery for Massine's ballet *Les Présages*
1934	Short stay in Paris. Lives in Tossa (Catalonia) until outbreak of the Spanish Civil War in 1936; then again in Paris
1937	Scenery for Miguel de Cervantes' *Numance* at the Théâtre Antoine, directed by Jean-Louis Barrault. Stays in Brittany
1937–43	*Metamorphoses* series
1938	Scenery for Armand Salacrou's *La terre est ronde* at the Théâtre de l'Atelier, directed by Charles Dullin. Stays at Arcachon (Gironde)
1938–40	*Mythology of Nature* series
1939	Scenery for *La faim*, after Knut Hamsun, at the Théâtre de l'Atelier, directed by Jean-Louis Barrault
1940	Scenery for Cherubini's opera *Medea* at the Grand Opéra, directed by Charles Dullin
1941	March: travels by way of Martinique and the Antilles to the United States. Lives in or near New York City until 1945

1943	*Trees* series
1944	*The Encounters of the Chimera* series
1945	November: returns to France. Henceforth lives in Paris and Aix-en-Provence
1946	Scenery for *Hamlet* at the Théâtre Marigny, directed by Jean-Louis Barrault
1947	"Twenty-two drawings on the theme of Desire" series
1951	Lives in Venice
1952	Lives in Rome
1959	First showing of Jean Grémillon's color film of 1957, *Masson and the Four Elements*
1963	Scenery for Alban Berg's opera *Wozzeck* at the Grand Opéra, Paris, directed by Jean-Louis Barrault

Exhibitions

1924	Galerie Simon, Paris
1925	Surrealist exhibition at the Galerie Pierre, Paris
1926	Exhibition with Braque and Gris at the Galerie Jeanne Bucher, Paris; Künstlerhaus, Vienna
1929	Galerie Simon, Paris
1932	Paul Rosenberg Gallery, New York; Rosenberg & Helft Gallery, London; "Paris 1932" exhibition at the Nationalmuseum, Stockholm; Pierre Matisse Gallery, New York
1933	Galerie Jeanne Bucher, Paris
1934	Galerie Simon, Paris
1935	Pierre Matisse Gallery, New York
1936	Wildenstein Gallery, London; "Douze Peintres" exhibition at the Paul Rosenberg Gallery, New York; "Espagne 1934–1936" exhibition at the Galerie Simon, Paris
1938	Mayor Gallery, London
1941	The Baltimore Museum of Art
1942	Buchholz Gallery, New York
1944	Paul Rosenberg Gallery, New York; Buchholz Gallery, New York
1945	Buchholz Gallery, New York; Galerie Louise Leiris, Paris
1946	Galerie de la Pléiade, Paris; APIAW, Liége; Palais des Beaux-Arts, Brussels
1947	The Arts Council of Great Britain, London; Waddington Gallery, Dublin; Buchholz Gallery, New York; Galerie Louise Leiris, Paris; Vendôme, Paris
1948	Galerie Louise Leiris, Paris
1949	Kunstverein, Freiburg/Breisgau; Kestner-Gesellschaft, Hanover; Curt Valentin Gallery, New York; Galerie La Hune, Paris; The Baltimore Museum of Art
1950	Exhibition with Alberto Giacometti at the Kunsthalle, Basel; Galerie Louise Leiris, Paris
1951	Galerie Garibaldi, Marseilles
1952	Galerie Louise Leiris, Paris

1953	Paul Rosenberg Gallery, New York, Curt Valentin Gallery, New York; University of Louisville, Kentucky
1954	Galerie Louise Leiris, Paris; Traveling exhibition in Germany "Das graphische Werk von André Masson – Radierungen und Lithographien, 1942 bis 1952"
1955	The Leicester Galleries, London; Traveling exhibition in Germany "André Masson – Gemälde, Zeichnungen"
1957	"Peintures récentes et anciennes" exhibition at the Galerie Louise Leiris, Paris; Galerie Der Spiegel, Cologne; Galerie Rudolf Hoffmann, Hamburg
1958	Edgardo Acosta Gallery, Beverly Hills, California; Meiji Shobo, Tokyo; Marlborough Galleries, London; The Albertina, Vienna; Kunst-Kabinett Klihm, Munich; Saidenberg Gallery, New York; Galerie Furstenberg, Paris
1959	Galleria L'Attico, Rome; Galleria La Bussola, Turin; Galleria Bergamini, Milan
1960	Galleria Il Segno, Rome; Svensk-Franska Konstgalleriet, Stockholm; "Dessins 1922–1960" exhibition at the Galerie Louise Leiris, Paris
1961	Saidenberg Gallery, New York; Richard Feigen Gallery, Chicago
1962	"Peintures 1960–1961" exhibition at the Galerie Louise Leiris, Paris; Marlborough Fine Art, London
1963	"Le monde imaginaire d'André Masson, eaux-fortes et lithographies, 1934–1963" exhibition at the Galerie Gerald Cramer, Geneva
1964	Saidenberg Gallery, New York

Selected Bibliography

Barrault, Bataille, Breton, Desnos, Eluard, Guerne, Jouve, Landsberg, Leiris, Limbour, Péret. *André Masson*, with drawings by Masson (no publisher or place of publication indicated), 1940

Bousquet, Joë; Eluard, Paul; Leiris, Michel. *Hommage à André Masson*, Cahiers du Sud, 1929

Breton, André. "Prestige d'André Masson," *Le Minotaure*, 1939

Charbonnier, Georges. *Entretiens avec Georges Charbonnier*, preface by Georges Limbour, Paris, Julliard, 1958

Juin, Hubert. *André Masson*, Paris, Le Musée de Poche, 1963

Leiris, Michel; Limbour, Georges. *André Masson et son univers*, Paris, Editions des Trois Collines, 1947

Limbour, Georges. *Masson: Dessins*, Paris, Editions Braun, 1951

Pia, Pascal. *André Masson*, Paris, N. R. F., 1930

Sartre, Jean-Paul. *André Masson: 22 dessins sur le thème du désir*, Paris, Fernand Mourlot, 1962

The publishers wish to thank the Galerie Louise Leiris, Paris, who supplied the illustrations for the black-and-white plates. Ektachromes for the colorplates were made by Photo Routhier, Paris; John D. Schiff, New York; and Walter Steinkopf, Berlin.

Translated from the French by Robert Erich Wolf
Library of Congress Catalog Card Number: 65–19564

List of Plates